# Beyond Stranger Bridgerland

John E Olsen

Copyright © 2018 John Olsen

All rights reserved.

ISBN:
ISBN-13: 978-1721687312

# DEDICATION

This book is dedicated to my children, Cody, Mallory, and Colton. Never give up on your dreams.

# CONTENTS

| | Acknowledgments | i |
|---|---|---|
| 1 | Intro Grandmas Snowman | 3 |
| 2 | Wagon Train | 7 |
| 3 | Old Tools | 9 |
| 4 | Old Rock Church | 15 |
| 5 | Twin Falls Ghost | 19 |
| 6 | Kevin & the Shadow man | 25 |
| 7 | ISU Ghost | 27 |
| 8 | Lost Pioneer Boy | 31 |
| 9 | Grandma Ann's Visit | 33 |
| 10 | Last Motorcycle | 35 |
| 11 | UFO Snowstorm | 39 |
| 12 | Tincup UFO | 41 |
| 13 | Trolled on MT Naomi | 45 |
| 14 | Not My Cousin | 49 |
| 15 | Ridge Watchers | 53 |
| 16 | Pilot Mountain Monster | 57 |
| 17 | Skinwalker | 59 |
| 18 | Smiling Man | 61 |
| 19 | Late Night Visitor | 65 |
| 20 | Halloween in Wellsville | 67 |

| 21 | Lights Outhouse | 69 |
| 22 | Golfing With Bigfoot | 71 |
| 23 | Wellsville Mountain Monster | 75 |
| 24 | Black Eyed at Midnight | 79 |
| 24 | Glitches in the Matrix | 83 |
| 25 | Bear Lake | 91 |
| 26 | Hardware Ranch Lost Gold | 95 |

# ACKNOWLEDGMENTS

I'd like to Thank Annie Olsen, and Kim Walker, for their help in editing this book.

Also, to all those who have shared their stories…

John E Olsen

# INTRO
# &
# GRANDMAS SNOWMAN

I grew up in a house that was very paranormally active. So, I got used to odd and unexplainable things happening.

Sharing my stories with others opened the door to experiences others would then share with me. By the age of 17, I interviewed and investigated other people's interactions with the paranormal.

The spirit that lived in my home was a bit of a prankster. Over my lifetime, I'd become very accustomed to things moving or going missing. There aren't too many things that happen around the house that rattle me.

My own kids have grown up spending a lot of time at their Grandparent's house. My mother watched them a couple of times a week while my wife and I went to work. Over the years, they have seen some strange things as well. My oldest son Cody has become a target for the ghost's attention. I'm not sure why, but he enjoys picking on Cody more than the other grandkids.

One object the ghost loved to manipulate was Grandma's Snowman. I don't remember exactly where my mother got it, but it was about 4 feet tall, and inside the white 'snow' padding, it was made with heavy dowels to help hold it upright. There was a sandbag base, so it was pretty heavy and hard to move around. Every year during the holidays, it sat in the front room. It was placed in a particular corner, but it never liked to stay there. Somehow, at night or when my parents were away, the ghost would move it around the front room. The person that noticed it the most was my son Cody. It really bothered him to see that it had moved, especially on those nights when he slept over. After Christmas, the snowman was always placed in a storage room in the basement so that it would be out of the way.

Grandpa hired Cody to paint the stairwell and hallway leading to the basement one spring. He'd been painting for some time and had already made his way down the stairs. Cody had just started working in the little hallway adjacent to the storage room. He had his earphones in, listening to music while he worked. Cody was moving right along when suddenly, a creepy feeling came over him. He stopped and looked into the storage room. There, in the corner, was the snowman staring at him. He really didn't like this. So, he walked across the room, picked up the snowman, and placed it in the corner. He made sure to turn it away from the door, facing the back wall of the storage room.

Feeling a bit better, he went back to his music and painting. After about 10 min, he felt uneasy again. He poked his head around the corner to peer into the storage room. Right in the middle of the room was the snowman staring at him. Not only had it turned around, but it had moved 6 feet to the middle of the room. Cody ran upstairs and told us what had happened. In no uncertain terms, he let us know that he would not finish the painting until the snowman was gone.

With Grandma's permission, I took the snowman to the front porch. It stayed there until grandma sold it a few weeks later. I hope the ghost didn't leave with it when it was sold.

## WAGON TRAIN
### BY AVERI

My mother and I had spent the day in Salt Lake City shopping. We enjoy the trip a couple of times a year together. As we headed back to Cache Valley up to the Sardine Canyon, the sun had just set behind the mountains, and the valley was in a beautiful red glow.

My mother was driving, and we talked about our fun day as we headed past Wellsville, nearing Logan. We had just passed the Historical Farm when I noticed something very odd in the fields to our right. I told Mom to slow down as we approached a field on the east side of the road. In a row just inside the area, there was a wagon train of about ten wagons. It was getting pretty dark, but in the last light of the day, I could see everyone was dressed in early period clothes, and a few wagons even had some milk cows tied to the back. As we slowed down, I could also see kids running alongside the carriages. I could see barrels tied on the side of the wagons. It looked very authentic to what I had read.

After we passed, I told my mom I wanted to go back. I had my camera with me and wanted to take a picture. I assumed that something was going on at the American West Historical Farm. We got to the turn-off for Nibley and headed back to the field with the wagon train. We drove back to Wellsville but saw nothing. Confused, we again turned around and went to where I knew we had seen the wagons, but nothing was there.
On our way home, we talked about what we had seen and questioned where they could have gone in such a short time. The description of what we each saw matched up, but it had vanished. The next day I called the American West Center, but they said that there had been no activities that day. They had no idea what I was talking about. I thanked them and hung up. It wasn't until that moment that I realized what we had seen was something from out of our time, a scene that hadn't taken place for over a hundred years.

I feel blessed to have seen this small piece of history for myself.

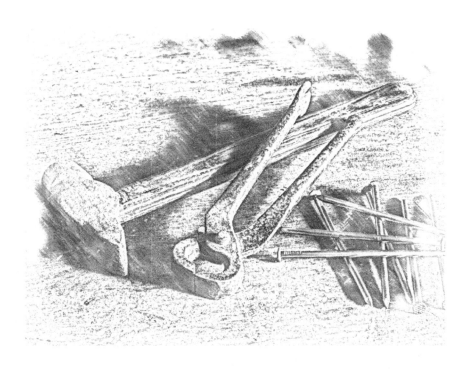

## OLD TOOLS
### BY TIFFANY

I've always loved decorating with beautiful old objects. I love rustic things. When my husband and I finished our new home in West Logan in 2002, I was so excited to decorate my new home. We had three kids at the time, ages 5, 3, and 18 months. We lived in a small two-bedroom apartment, and the new bigger space was very welcome.

I had the house finally put together with all of the children's rooms done, but the front sitting room didn't feel complete. It was a rustic theme with frames and shelves built from barn wood and a beautiful stand to hold my old knick-knacks. I had an old upright piano, given to me by my grandmother, that sat nicely in one corner. I liked how it all came together, but it felt like something was missing.

One day my mother and I were in town shopping, and I talked her into stopping at a small antique shop. I love looking through antiques. I could have spent all day looking over the shop, but my mother was not as excited to be there. I was looking around when a leather bag caught my eye. I pulled it out, thinking it was an old doctor's bag, but it was heavier than it appeared. It was tattered black leather with the name "Schubert" on the side engraved in gold, with worn letters. Inside the bag, I found a hammer and other tools. There were some in there that I had never seen before. I had no idea what they might have been used for. I instantly fell in love with it and felt it would go great on my shelf to complete my decor. I bought it at a reasonable price and took it home. After a thorough cleaning, I set the bag up with some of the tools sitting out on the shelf. After a bit of research, I found that an old shoe cobbler used the tools.

One day about a week after I set them out, I came into the sitting room and found all the tools had been placed back in the bag. I asked my husband if he had put them away, but he hadn't done it. I didn't think my 5-year-old son could have reached them, so I took them out and set them back up. Two days later, I woke to find the bag packed once again. Confused, I asked my 5-year-old, but he said he hadn't touched them. Again, I set them out very puzzled. The tool movement continued off and on for a couple of months. I was beginning to think someone was playing a prank on me.

One night my husband and I were lying in bed. I was reading, and he was almost asleep. Suddenly, I heard my 18-month-old daughter start to whimper over the baby monitor. I listened intently; we were trying to let her fuss so she could learn to go back to sleep by herself. As I listened to her whine, I heard something else come through the monitor. It was a deep male voice singing softly! I bolted upright in bed. The sound was faint but definitely a deep male voice singing something like a lullaby, but I didn't recognize the words or language. I woke up my husband, and we both ran down the hall. We opened the door, and I scooped up my daughter. We searched the room and then the house but didn't find anything out of the ordinary. My husband thought maybe it was a crossed signal on the baby monitor. I wasn't so sure. A few nights later, the same thing happened again. I made my husband search again, and he found nothing. I started to think he might have been right about the crossed signal. Maybe it was picking up sounds from another source. I just found it strange that it only started when my daughter started to fuss. I began to think that might have been in my head as well.

One afternoon, I cleaned the kitchen while my oldest was at preschool. My youngest was taking a nap, and my 3-year-old son played quietly in the sitting room. Suddenly, I realized my 3-year-old son was talking to someone. I could hear him talking. I thought he might be talking to himself -- which wouldn't be strange for a 3-year-old --, but then I listened to a man's voice answer. I stopped what I was doing and listened intently from the kitchen. I couldn't catch the words, but my son was laughing and talking, and I heard a deep male voice talk back again. I walked into the sitting room, expecting to find someone there but found just my son. I asked him who he was talking to. He answered, "It's just the grandpa man, " Without looking up from his toys."

I walked over, sat on the couch, and pulled him onto my lap. I asked him who the grandpa man was. He explained that he was an old man that talked to him. I asked what he looked like, but all he would say was he had a gray mustache and a hat like a grandpa. I was beginning to get very concerned. I had never experienced anything like this and had always believed people who told ghost stories were exaggerating. Now, I was not so sure. The incidents seemed to come in waves. It would calm down for a few weeks, just long enough for us to think it was over, then it would start up again.

It all came to a head one late night, six months after I brought the bag home from the antique store. My husband and I woke to a loud, banging noise coming from the sitting room. It sounded like things were being moved around the room. We both jumped out of bed and walked down to the front room. We stopped at the entrance, both staring through the doorway. The old bag was thrown on the floor, and tools were strewn across the floor. Standing next to scatter antiques was an older gentleman. He was almost completely solid but still slightly see-through. He was tall with a stout build. He wore an old flat cabbie hat, old-world wool shirt, and homespun pants. His face was lined and sad with a bushy grey mustache. He was looking at the tools on the floor. After a short time, he realized we were watching him. He looked up with a sad smile, and then he faded. He was gone. At this point, I realized I hadn't taken a breath since I had stepped out of bed.

My husband quickly swept the tools up into the bag and took them to the garage.

The next day, I looked through the tools in the bag and set them on the table. Honestly, I was torn on what to do. I didn't want this in my house, but I also would not leave them in the garage. These tools represented someone's life's work. It made sense that he might have chosen to stay with them. I held on to the tools for a few days, but I finally concluded I needed to get them out of the house. I took them back to the antique shop, and without explaining too much, I asked if I could return them. They took them back with a restocking fee out of the price. I hope the old man found peace.

## OLD ROCK CHURCH
### BY CRAG

My wife and I were celebrating our wedding anniversary. We wanted to stay close to home but still get away for the night. We packed up the kids, dropped them off at my sister-in-law's house, and headed out. It was a chilly autumn day. We had dinner at the Copper Mill, then walked around town. Around 8 pm, we got to The Old Rock Church in Providence, where we had a room for the night.

After a beautiful quiet evening, we settled in to get some shut-eye.

At around 2 am, my wife woke me up and asked if I could hear someone talking. I was dead asleep and had heard nothing. We sat quietly, listening for about 5 minutes in complete silence. I was about to turn over and go back to sleep when I suddenly heard whispers. I had to strain to hear, but it was undeniable that a man and woman were talking in our room. They were very upset about something. At first, I thought it must be coming from another suite, but it was definitely coming from inside our room after listening further.

The hair stood up on the back of my neck as I reached over to turn on the light. The whispering halted as the room lit up, and the room was utterly silent. My wife was distraught and wanted to leave at once. After a few moments, I convinced her it was just someone in the hallway, and she had nothing to worry about. In truth, I knew exactly what it was. Two spirits talked about us in the same room where we slept. I shut off the light, and we lay awake in bed for a long time. After there were no more sounds for a long time, we drifted back to sleep.

It must have been an hour later when I woke with a quick jerk like someone had grabbed me. Something had poked me. My wife was still asleep, breathing heavily behind me. I strained to look around in the dark, figuring out what had startled me awake. Suddenly my blood ran cold when I saw a woman in a dark dress silhouetted by the streetlight coming in from the window. My eyes cleared from the sleepiness as adrenaline rushed through my veins. She was wearing a long dress that went to the floor and a light bonnet on her head. Her arms crossed over her chest, and she had a stern, unhappy look on her face. As I continued to stare in fear and disbelief, she shook her head at me in disgust. I fumbled for the light switch. I turned my head for a split second to see where to turn on the light. Again, I turned the light on and looked back to find that she was gone. I lay in bed, dumbstruck. After a few moments, I laid back in bed, shaking. I decided not to wake my wife but was determined NOT to turn the light off again. I was unable to sleep for the rest of the night.

We packed early and headed over to pick up the kids the following day. It was a month or so before I told my wife what I had seen. I've been back to the Old Rock Church three times since that night and have not had another sighting. Maybe that night was a fluke, but I know that night someone was not happy we had stayed.

### TWIN FALLS GHOST
#### BY KATE

My husband and I have good friends in Twin Falls, Idaho. Norm and Jill have been our friends for many years. My husband and Norm were in college together and met at USU back in the '70s. Even though we live 150 miles apart, we always spend a few weekends together every year, either at their place or at our home.

We have loved visiting them, but their house always seems a little off to me. They live in an old farmhouse they had restored. I never said anything to them, but I always felt like I was being watched.

One summer weekend, we dropped the kids off with my mother and headed to Twin Falls for a visit. We arrived around noon and brought our bags to the guest room. After visiting for a bit, we headed out for a day of sightseeing and headed off to dinner.

We played games and socialized into the wee hours of the morning. By the time we went to bed, I could barely keep my eyes open long enough to get ready for bed. My head hardly hit the pillow, and I was out cold. Around 3 am, I woke to the sound of a squeaky door. My husband was snoring loudly and didn't wake up. I looked up to see where the noise was coming from. The entrance to the closet was slowly opening. It was a small walk-in closet with an old heavy wood door. It has always been creaky but has never opened on its own. I stared for a while into the black of the open closet and saw movement. I couldn't make out much, but there was a shape inside. I reached over and turned on the bedside light. When I did, all I could see was clothes, nothing else. I woke up my husband and begged him to check the closet. I pulled the covers up to my nose and waited for him to report. Groggy from sleep, he reluctantly got up to check it out, but he didn't find anything. He closed the door and went back to bed. He fell back to sleep right away. It took a while for me to fall asleep, but I eventually did.

When I awoke in the morning, the light was starting to fill the room. I rolled over and opened my eye. The first thing I was the closet door. It was wide open! I hit my husband on the arm, and he grunted and looked up. I asked him if he had opened the closet door. He swore up and down that he didn't open it. He likes to play pranks on me from time to time.

I shrugged off the eerie feeling and got ready for the day. We had a great day with Norm and Jill. We visited with their family and did some more sightseeing. We finished the day with a great meal that Jill and I cooked with fresh ingredients from the garden.

We stayed up again, talking and playing games. We planned to get up reasonably early Sunday morning and head home. We headed to bed a bit earlier than the night before, and I fell asleep quickly. I was tired from the day and my interrupted sleep the night before. I made sure to shut the closet door tightly right before going to bed.

Once again, I woke up at around 3 am to the creaking of the closet door. I was facing my husband, and even though I was now fully awake, I didn't move. I lay quietly and as still as I could with my heart pounding in my chest. I heard faint footsteps coming out of the closet. They seemed to walk from the closet to my side of the bed. I tried to wake my husband by gently poking his back, but he wouldn't come out of his deep sleep. Slowly, I turned and looked at the closet. Sure enough, it was open. I knew I needed to turn over the rest of the way to reach the light, so I slowly started shifting.

That's when I saw her. She was standing at the side of my bed, leaning over me. It was an older woman in a vintage pioneer dress. Her hair was under an old-style bonnet. Her face was close, only 2 feet from mine! I noticed that she had a wicked smile on her face that didn't reach her eyes. When our eyes met, she started laughing at me. There was no sound, but she continued to stare at me and laughing. I was frozen with fear, and I couldn't move a muscle. She continued to look down at me with her silent laugh. Finally, I reached behind me and grabbed my husband's leg. I squeezed as hard as I could until he jumped with a yell. He flipped on the light, and the woman immediately disappeared. I instantly burst into tears, shaking uncontrollably. My husband held me as I wept until I calmed down and could tell him what had happened.

After I calmed down enough to speak, he asked if I wanted to go back to sleep. I told him that under no circumstance was I staying even five more minutes. We quickly tossed all our stuff in the car and left. We called from the road a little later and explained I was feeling very ill and needed to go home. I wondered if I should tell them the truth but thought better of it.

We didn't revisit them at that house. They sold it three years after that last visit. I felt terrible, but how do you tell someone they have a ghost living in the closet that hates you?

## KEVEN AND THE SHADOWMAN
### BY KEVEN

I grew up in Smithfield in the '60s. Back then, it was a much smaller place than it is now. My friends and I ran around town late into the evenings. We had many great adventures living in this small community. We always felt very safe in our neighborhood.

I first became interested in the paranormal when I saw something I couldn't explain one night. The first time I personally saw it, I woke up in the middle of the night, and something was standing at the end of my bed. I could see through it, but it had a definition and outline of a man. When I turned on my light, it disappeared. After explaining what I'd seen to my friends, we began calling it the "Shadow Man."

After that, we searched to see if we could find it again. My friends and I would catch glimpses of him walking in different places late at night. He was in the form of a dark shadow, much darker than the night. He would disappear as he approached the streetlights, only to reappear in the darkness on the other side.

Over time, I sensed that the Shadow Man knew we could see him. One night, around dusk, my friends and I were riding our skateboards when my friend Jason was pushed off his board as we skated down the road. We looked in the direction from which he was shoved to see the shadow man running away from us. We chased him only to have him disappear before our eyes.

One evening, my friends and I rode our bikes around town past dark. We saw the Shadow Man and followed him. We couldn't catch up to him as hard as we tried, and he lost us in the cemetery. We sat on our bicycles, straining to see where he might have gone. Then, we heard a sound behind us. We turned quickly to see him standing right behind us. The Shadow Man freaked us out. We left as quickly as possible, hoping he would not follow us.

I often wonder if he is still roaming around in Smithfield to this day.

Later, I lived in a home I knew was haunted. I lived there for many years and experienced a lot of unexplainable things. Open doors would shut by themselves, and you could often hear footsteps when no one was there. They varied from boots stomping up and down the hallway to quiet 'stepping' creaks across the ceiling coming from the upstairs rooms. These oddities always seemed to happen when you were alone.

Since that time, I have spent many hours investigating paranormal hot spots in the Valley. I've located a few places in the mountain ranges of Cache Valley where people have experienced the feeling of being watched, stalked, or even run off by strange ghostly phenomena. I've witnessed some unexplainable things near the state sheds in Sardine Canyon, Providence Canyon's top, and in Green Canyon above North Logan. I continue to investigate the paranormal to this day.

### ISU GHOST
#### BY JILL

I had just graduated from high school, and I was excited to be preparing to go to college. I decided to go to Idaho State near my home in Pocatello, Idaho. I grew up about 30 miles outside Pocatello and was looking forward to being close to home but out on my own.

One of the main reasons I chose ISU was that freshmen were not required to live on campus. Not living on campus fit my situation well because I didn't have enough money to live in a dorm. Pretty quickly, I found an ad looking for a roommate. It was a great price and wasn't too far off-campus. I applied to live there and was excited as I drove over to see it. I found an old Victorian-style home with three levels when I got there. I met my future roommates as well, and they seemed nice. It would be three other girls in the house and me. They were all attending ISU as well. My bedroom was going to be on the 3rd floor. I was the newest person there, so I got the smallest room. Having a small space didn't dampen my spirits; I was ecstatic! I was going to college, and I was entirely independent for the first time.

I moved in the Thursday just before school started, and I had spent the day setting up my room and getting to know a few of the girls. That night I was exhausted. I practically fell into bed and slept soundly through the night.

The next night, something strange happened. I was in bed reading when I heard heavy steps walking down the hall. It sounded like big boots pounding on the hard floor with each step. It roamed down the hall towards my room and stopped just outside my door. I waited for a knock, thinking it was one of my roommates, but there was no sound. I got up and opened the door expecting someone to be there, but there was nothing. I shook it off and went back to reading. A short time later, the boot steps started again, walking away from my door and back down the hall. I sat quietly for what felt like forever but didn't hear the boots again that night. The loud footsteps would wake me up 2 or 3 times a week for the next couple of weeks.

I finally asked Nat (one of my roommates) if she had ever heard the boots. She was quiet for a moment, and then she told me the girl who was renting the room before I did, left because she said the house was too haunted for her. I asked if she had heard anything. She admitted she had but reassured me. She told me I shouldn't worry about it. She said, "He wouldn't hurt you." Then smiled weakly and walked out.

After a while, I started to get used to the sounds at night. I justified that it was just an old house. Besides, I signed a contract through the end of the school year, and there was no getting out of it.

The footsteps became almost normal, and they didn't even wake me up much anymore. But then things escalated, and my stuff started to move and disappear. One morning my hairbrush was missing. I went through everything in my room looking for it. I finally gave up and grabbed my backpack to head to school. When I opened my door to leave, my brush was sitting on the floor right outside my door. I thought maybe Nat or one of the other girls borrowed it, but when I asked them, they said none of them had borrowed it.

Another day, I woke up for school, and all my books had been taken out of my bag and tossed around my room. What scared me most was that the sound of my stuff being thrown around never woke me up.

I remember one winter afternoon when I was alone in the house. I was down in the living room when I saw movement out of the corner of my eye. I saw someone walk down the stairs and into the front room. I watched TV intently and just said: "Hey, I thought you left already?" But they didn't answer. So, I turned to look at them, but no one was there. I know I saw a form walk down the stairs and into the front room! I got my coat and quickly left; I wasn't staying there alone that day.

Soon after that, there was yet another incident that frightened me. I woke up in the middle of the night to the sound of someone knocking on my door. I got up, thinking it was one of my roommates. I opened the door to find the hall empty. Tired and confused, I shuffled back to bed. Just as I put my head back on my pillow, "BANG! BANG! BANG!" the knocking came louder. I turned on the light and opened the door; no one was there. At this point, I was done! In a firm voice, I said, "I am not leaving; I am not afraid of you! I live here, and you will NOT bother me anymore!" I closed the door and went back to bed.

The rest of the year, things were a little better. Things would be "quiet" for a few weeks, then act up again. I would give a firm speech about leaving me alone, and things would quiet down again.

At the end of my contract, I moved out. I know with certainty that I lived with a ghost for a year. I do not doubt that what I experienced was paranormal.

## LOST PIONEER BOY
### BY ANDY

I grew up in Cache Valley in the '70s in a family that loved the outdoors. I hunted and fished with my older brothers throughout my childhood. At the time, I had never really put much stock into ghost stories. I didn't think much about it until one day in October when I was 16 years old.

It was the first year I could carry a rifle and hunt deer. My older brother was 19, and he and I had been hunting for a week without much success. We had decided to go hunting in Scare Canyon; Scare Canyon is located between Ant Flats and Porcupine Dam in the Cache National forest. Back then, we hunted in this area south of hardware Ranch, but I believe most of the land today is private property. We had hunted all day and passed up a few small bucks hoping for a shot at a bigger one. As the afternoon turned into dusk, we sat at the top of the canyon, just watching over the gorge, hoping to find a giant buck.

It was almost too dark to see when I heard a strange sound coming from the brush and trees down to our left. I looked at my brother, and he signaled that he could hear it too. It was quiet at first, but soon I could hear it very clearly. It was a young boy crying! We jumped up and headed down the trail in the direction of the cry. Since noon, we hadn't seen anyone and hadn't seen any kids all day. What was a kid doing up here? I thought to myself. I kept up with my brother as we weaved our way through the brush and trees-following the sound of the sobbing. My mind raced as my brother and I entered the scrub. In front of us, crouched down, was a boy about 8 or 9 years old. He cried while hugging his knees to his chest and his face buried in his chest.

The first thing that struck me was his clothing. He had on an old hand-sewn shirt and ragged overalls. He wore no shoes, and his feet were black with dirt. As we caught our breath, my brother called out to him to see if he was ok. He looked up at us, and in the fading light, I could see his blue eyes under his ragged brown hair. I could see tear streaks running down his filthy cheeks. He looked as though he was lost for a long time. He looked at us and then slowly pointed to our right. I strained to look at what he was trying to show us, but when I looked back, he had disappeared. I froze! All I could hear was the sound of pulsing blood in my ears. After what felt like an eternity of staring at the spot where the boy had just been, my brother slapped my shoulder, and we headed out of the brush at a run. I snapped out of it and ran with him all the way back to our car. It was dark and late by the time we headed back to town. Every time I tried to talk to my brother about what we had seen, he would tell me to shut up and tell me that he didn't want to talk about it.

It was years before we talked about it again. When we did, my brother told me precisely what he had seen, and it perfectly matched my memory of the event. I don't know who that boy was or what he was pointing at, but I never hunted in Scare Canyon again. The boy has been my only ghost encounter, and it's one I'll never forget.

## GRANDMA ANN'S VISIT
### BY JOHN

It was an early Saturday morning; my wife was already up and gone for work. She usually worked early on Saturdays. She had just left, so only my son and I were in the house. I was lying in bed, deciding whether to go back to sleep or get up. I was somewhere between being awake and asleep, but my son was still sleeping in his room on the other side of the house.

The next thing I remember, there was a knock on my bedroom door. Half asleep, I mumbled, "come in," with a groggy voice. The door opened, and it was my Grandma Ann, my Mother's Mom. She came in and sat down on the edge of my bed. I hadn't seen my Grandma in quite a while. She smiled, and we had a long conversation about how she was doing and what the family was doing. She asked how my Mom was doing, and then suddenly, I stopped and looked at her. I was starting to wake up enough to realize what I was seeing...

I said, "Grandma, you passed away."

She smiled and said, "That doesn't mean I can't come to visit from time to time." With that comment, she smiled, said goodbye, and walked out the door.

As I slowly came to my full senses, I started looking for

evidence of what had happened. I looked at the spot where she had sat on the bed, and the imprint of where she had sat was still there.

Six months earlier, my Grandma Ann, who lived in Denmark, had packed her suitcase to take a flight to come to visit us. Feeling tired, she laid down on the couch in her front room and passed away. At the time, I didn't have the money to go to Denmark for the funeral. I hadn't felt the closure I needed until that morning when Grandma came to say goodbye six months later.

## LAST MOTORCYCLE
### BY JOHN

I have always loved motorcycles, and I have always owned one since I was a teenager. When I was in my early 20's, my uncle sold me his 1985 Honda 550cc in mint condition. It was 20 years old with less than 500 miles on it. I was so excited to own this bike. At the time, I was married, and we had one son, who was three years old.

It was spring when I bought the bike, and I rode it everywhere. I'd only had it two months when I was hit by a car. The lady in the car hadn't seen me and pulled into my lane, hitting me head-on. I always wore my helmet, and even though the bike was demolished, miraculously, I only separated three ribs. I was upset at the loss of my bike, but after a few months, the lady's insurance paid to replace it.

I was taking my time to find the perfect replacement motorcycle. I looked at quite a few, but none of the bikes felt right. One afternoon, my family and I headed to the grocery store to do a little shopping at the old Macey's shopping center in Logan, Utah. It was the old store before they built the new one in Providence. As we walked in, I got an odd feeling. There weren't many people shopping, and I looked around as I put my son in the shopping cart. At the end of one of the aisles, I saw a man I didn't recognize. He had on a gray T-shirt and Levi's and intently stared at me. I smiled, nodded, and continued with my shopping. As we shopped, I occasionally caught glimpses of the man staring at me. I felt kind of uncomfortable but didn't say anything. I didn't want to upset my wife or son.

The three of us were almost done shopping. We just had milk and cereal left, so my wife headed to get milk, and I took the cart to grab the cereal. I told her I would meet her at the register. I was looking at the cereal, trying to decide on a cereal box, when I felt someone behind me. I turned to see the same man from earlier standing right in front of my son, sitting in the cart. I turned, smiled at him, and nodded a hello. Now that he was closer, I noticed his shirt and Levi's were dirty and a little ripped. He had a road rash on his arm. It looked like the man had just been in an accident. He looked from me to my son and smiled.

"You have a beautiful family," he said to me. I smiled and said, "Thank you." Then he looked back at me, his face turning grave. "I had a family once," he continued, "but I don't get to see them anymore since the accident." Hearing this made my blood run ice cold in my veins. In a profound and convincing voice, he stared at me and said, "You should not buy another motorcycle. Do you understand what I'm telling you?" I knew this was not just a stranger sharing a story; this was a warning in my soul. "Yes," was all I could get out. He smiled, looked at my son, then walked down the aisle and was gone.

I followed him down the aisle, but I knew what I would see before I got to the end of the aisle. I couldn't find the man anywhere. I met my wife at the register and checked out; in the car asked if she had seen the man. She didn't know who I was talking about.

I thought it over for days, but in the end, I couldn't deny the warning I was given; I was not to buy another bike.
It's been 17 years, and I have never purchased another motorcycle. I miss riding very much, and I think about it a lot. I believe the man I met in the store was warning me. He was a kind spirit who didn't want me to face his fate.

## UFO SNOWSTORM
### BY JOE

It was mid-November in 1996, and my wife and I had traveled to Pocatello, Idaho, for a family wedding. We left early in the morning in clear, cold weather. A storm was supposed to arrive before the next day, so we planned to travel back to Utah that same night, right after the festivities.

The day was filled with last-minute preparations for the wedding and a beautiful ceremony. The reception ended in the afternoon, and it was all food and fun. It started to near about 9 o'clock when I was finally able to pry my wife from the party. I know it was a couple of hours drive to get home, and I wanted to get a good start before the storm.

Just as we left Pocatello, the storm made an early arrival. It was a full-on blizzard by the time we had left the freeway and headed past Downy Idaho. It was becoming increasingly more challenging to see the road, and I moved at a snail's pace. A few hours later, we reached the area between Swan Lake and Preston, Idaho. This area is nothing but farmland and sagebrush with some gullies here and there. As we traveled slowly South, I could see glowing lights off in the distance. As we got closer, it became apparent that it was something strange. I figured we must be coming up on an accident or a snowplow.

I came to a spot where there was a large gully. The ravine opened up more extensively as it flowed away from the road. Hovering in the gorge, less than 50 yards away from us, was a bright silver glowing craft. It appeared to be around 30 feet across and roughly 20 feet high. It had the appearance of a classic round dish shape UFO. It was silver and glowing. There were two lights on the top and one underneath. I came to a complete stop, and we stared at it for about 5 minutes. We could tell it was hovering even through the heavy snowfall, but there was no audible sound. I told my wife I wanted to get out for a better look. She grabbed my arm and said to me under no circumstance was I getting out. We watched for about five more minutes, and my wife demanded we leave. I really wanted to stay longer, but she was getting more upset, so I drove off. Right before we reached Preston, the snow had stopped, and we could travel the rest of the way back home safely.

When we walked into the house, I looked at the clock, and to my surprise, it was 4:30 am! I calculated the time, and it should have been only 1:00 am. I checked the clock on the TV, and sure enough, it was 4:30. Even traveling through the storm shouldn't have taken us more than 4-5 hours to get home, but it took us seven and a half hours! My wife and I talked about whether to tell anyone but decided to keep it to ourselves. I still can't piece together how we lost 3 hours.

## TINCUP UFO
### BY TRAVIS

When I was going to school in Rexburg, Idaho, I worked part-time as an auto parts delivery driver for an auto parts distribution company. I got paid mileage plus expenses and an hourly wage on top of that, so it wasn't too bad of a deal. I did deliveries all over Eastern Idaho, into Wyoming, and occasionally as far as West Yellowstone, Montana. It was mostly small parts that I ran around in my old beat-up truck. Most times, it was within a 40 or 50-mile radius. Longer runs only came up on occasion.

It was almost quitting time on a Thursday when my boss called me into his office. I was just about to head home for the evening. He told me he had an emergency drop-off in Jackson Hole, Wyoming. It was something that had to be delivered tonight. He said to me that if I ran this job tonight, I could have Friday off and that he would give me the money to spend the night in Jackson at a nice place. I agreed to do the delivery and loaded up the parts.

I planned to drop off the parts, grab a bite to eat then head to Soda Springs to see my family for the weekend. I would pocket the extra money my boss gave me for a hotel room and just sleep in the back of my truck if I got tired.

I stopped by my apartment, grabbed my bedroll, and headed towards Jackson Hole. My drive there was uneventful. I dropped off the parts, grabbed some dinner, then immediately fueled up and headed towards Soda Springs.

It was getting close to midnight when I started up Tincup canyon. Tincup is a small canyon with a weaving two-lane road. It usually did not have much traffic at this time of night. Halfway up the canyon, I found a turnoff where I could park my truck and sleep. It was near a small river and out of sight of the road. I untied my bedroll in the back of my vehicle and crawled into sleep. I was comfortable and felt secure; having a shell over the bed of my truck helped. In the high country, the shell would help keep the rain off if a shower came through at night. I was exhausted and fell right into a heavy sleep.

I was awakened sometime later by a deep hum that was vibrating the entire bed of my truck and the shell over my head. The deep hum made the aluminum shell bounce and creak all over. I opened my eyes, and a bright light came in the window. A fluorescent glow came in as if there were something in front of my truck.

I quickly slid out of my bedroll and out of my truck. I glanced toward the west. About 75 yards from me was a triangle-shaped ship hovering. It had a bright light at each point of the triangle and blue light at the bottom center. The blue light on the bottom of the craft was directed towards the creek. As my eyes adjusted, I was able to look closer. I noticed the beam of light pointing towards the water seemed shimmering. As I got a better look, I realized that this weird shimmer was water. The ship was pulling water out of the creek and up into the ship.

I stood frozen, just watching. After about 5 minutes, I wondered if I should jump into my truck and leave. But I couldn't move. I was in complete amazement at what I was seeing. Suddenly, the beam shut off, and the suspended water in the beam fell back down into the river with a splash. I realized everything around me was deadly quiet. The loud hum was gone, and even the forest was silent. I watched in amazement as the ship turned away from me and slowly moved towards the west. Then, it was gone in a flash of blue and white light.

I stood there shaking in the cold night air as all the nighttime sounds slowly returned. After a while, I regained my composure and got back in my truck. I sat for some time, thinking about what I'd seen. I firmly believe that what I saw was a UFO. I decided not to tell anyone; I figured anyone I told would think I was crazy. It's been ten years, and I've only shared my story with a few select people. After this experience, I've looked at the night sky very differently. I have wondered who was piloting the craft that night.

## TROLLED ON MT NAOMI
### BY BRAD

I moved to Cache Valley in the summer of 2002. I had visited a good friend going to school at Utah State and fell in love with the valley. I was single at the time, and in my early 20's, I loved the outdoors. Logan was perfect for me because it had rock climbing, hiking, camping, and great snow for snowboarding very close to town.

Early one fall day, a friend and I had decided to hike Mt Naomi. We planned to take a bedroll and simple cold food. We couldn't cook because there was a fire restriction at that time. The day came for us to head out when I got a call from my friend. He had a family emergency out of town and wouldn't be able to go. I decided I would go on my own. When you're in your 20s, you're invincible, and I wasn't afraid to hike and camp alone

It was a quiet Wednesday in September. As I pulled into the parking lot in Tony Grove, it was almost empty. There were a few vehicles and one trailer. I loaded up and hit the trail. It was a beautiful hike as I followed the path heading north. The walk begins at Tony Grove, which sits at 8,100 feet elevation and ends at 9,984 feet elevation at the top. The terrain at this elevation is mostly outcropping of granite rock and tall pines.

I took it easy, not pushing too hard. I knew I would spend the night and push on to the top the following day. I hiked until the sun began to sink in the west. I found a flat spot about 40 yards off the trail under a large pine. I ate my cold dinner while watching the sunset. When it got dark, I crawled into my sleeping bag and pulled out my headlamp and book. I always kept a paperback book to read in my pack. I read until I got tired, then laid in my bedroll and watched the stars until I fell asleep.

I awoke with a start in the middle of the night. As I came to my senses, I realized it was quiet; too quiet; no sounds at all. I am usually a deep sleeper, and it takes a lot to wake me, so I knew something had to have happened for me to wake up. I was very uneasy, which was also not like me. I've spent many nights camping alone without any problems. I knew bears and other animals were around, but I couldn't hear anything. I tried to calm down and sleep, but the unease I felt continued. Suddenly I heard a sound that I couldn't place. It was like a calling whistle. I racked my brain to think of any birds that sounded like that. I sat up in my bedroll and looked for my headlamp. I was about to give up when I was struck in the chest by a small rock. I froze, and I realized the whistle had stopped.

I quickly slipped my boots on as my mind whirled. Birds don't throw stones, and I couldn't imagine what was up here that could throw one. As I got my last boot on, I remembered that my lamp was still on my head, and I fumbled to turn it on.

I looked around to see what had thrown the rock when I froze. About 15 feet from me, sitting on a pile of exposed rock, was a creature. The figure was small, around 4' tall, crouched on its haunches. It had pale gray/green skin. Its features were close to a man's, but its ears and nose were longer and pointy. It was very bony and sickly looking. Even more strange, it was wearing a gray, worn-out shirt and ragged handmade pants.

I was in shock at what I was seeing. It was surreal as I took it in. The creature had big black eyes and a large mouth. As I sat trying to take it all in slowly, the creature got a broad smile on its face, and it leaned forward. Suddenly it whistled at me through its teeth. I looked down and realized it had my paperback book in its left hand and slowly slid it behind its back. It hit me like a bolt of lightning. If it had my book, it had been right next to me as I slept. The thought snapped me out of my trance, and fight-or-flight mode filled my body with adrenaline.

Scooping up my bedroll and grabbing my pack, I sprinted toward the trail. As I hit the trail, I tripped, throwing my stuff everywhere. I caught my breath and gathered all my belongings as I watched closely around me. I got everything shoved into my pack and put it on. I wrapped what was left of my bedroll over my backpack. I started heading down when I heard the whistle again, not far behind me. At that, I ran at a sprint down the trail.

The rest of the way back, I heard and saw nothing. I quickly loaded my truck and sat in my vehicle, trying to catch my breath and come to my senses. I drove home, questioning my sanity. I never camped alone again. I've been very selective to whom I have told this story. I have come to believe others might have seen this creature but will not share their story because it sounds crazy. I questioned my sanity for a long time after, but I knew what I saw was real.

Writers notes: Many Native American cultures have names for such creatures, as explained by Brad in his story.

The Pukwudgie: known in Native American lore, is native to America: a small, grey-faced, large-eared creature distantly related to the European goblin. Fiercely independent, tricky, and not over-fond of humankind, it possesses its own powerful magic. Pukwudgies hunt with deadly, poisonous arrows and enjoy playing tricks on humans.

## NOT MY COUSIN
### BY CHRIS

Growing up in Cache Valley, one of our family's favorite pastimes was camping. We often went with extended family and friends for weekend camping trips. Summers were so exciting as a kid spending weekends up at Bear Lake or Logan Canyon.

One summer weekend, my uncle's family and our family were camping in Logan Canyon near Temple Fork. I was 11 at the time, and one of my best friends was my cousin Trevor. Trevor was a year older than me, and I thought he was so cool. We did everything together during the summer.

Trevor and I had spent the whole day fishing and running around camp. We met some other kids our age from the campground just above us and had played football right before dinner. My mother called us to camp for supper, and we ate quickly. We wanted to play night games like the older kids, but our parents told us we had to be back before dark.

We got the other kids (there were 5 of us in all) and decided to play hide and seek. Trevor chose me to seek first, so I stayed at the trailer and counted. I took off and found two of the kids in the trees by the river and then headed for the small ravine where I thought Trevor might have gone. At the bottom of the ravine was a trail that headed up a small canyon. I was looking around when I heard someone laugh. About 40 yards up the path, I turned and saw Trevor sticking his head out from behind a tree. I yelled that I had found him, but he just smiled and waved me to come over to him. I walked up to the trail, and as I got about 10 yards away, my cousin disappeared behind the tree. I got to the large tree, and he was gone. Confused, I started to look around when I heard him laugh again. He was further up the trail behind another tree, poking his head out. Again, he motioned for me to follow him. I was a little annoyed, but I started up the path towards him. Once again, he ducked behind the tree and disappeared. I got to the tree, but he was nowhere to be found. I was about to head back down the trail when I saw him further up the trail. This time he was standing near a bend in the path, and he was still motioning me to follow as he walked around the corner. I got a bizarre feeling in the pit of my stomach, and I yelled for him to come back. He walked almost out of sight and stopped. He turned, and with a big smile, he waved for me to join him.

At this point, I was distraught. Trevor knew we were much further from camp than we should, and he still wanted to go on. It was getting late, and I did not want my dad to get after me. I yelled that I was going back, turned on my heels, and headed down the trail. I kept looking back, but I couldn't see if Trevor was following me or not. At this point, I realized I was much further up the canyon than I thought, so I picked up the pace. Before long, I was on a dead run. Something felt very off, and I wanted out of the canyon before dark.

As I ran into camp, I saw my mom roasting

marshmallows on sticks for all the kids. She demanded to know where I had been. I said I had been following Trevor up the trail, but I couldn't catch him. That's when I saw Trevor sitting in a chair roasting a marshmallow. I asked him how he beat me back to camp. Confused, Trevor explained how he had hidden under my dad's truck, and I had walked right by him. He had never left camp. My blood ran cold as I explained what had happened to me. Everyone laughed at me, but I insisted that I knew what I had seen. My mother told me Trevor had been there for over an hour, and she had seen him the whole time. Twenty-five years later, I still wonder who or what it was trying to get me up that canyon alone. I wonder if I would still be here if I had continued to follow it up that trail.

John E Olsen

# RIDGE WATCHERS
# BY CAM

I grew up on a small ranch in western Wyoming. Ever since I could walk, I helped on the ranch. As a family, the outdoors were our whole life; work and play, we were outside. As a little kid sitting around the fire after a hard day's work, I remember listening to my grandpa tell stories. He had so many great stories. He told us hunting and fishing stories, but some of my favorites were his encounters with the paranormal.

He talked about when he saw a UFO when he was feeding the cows one evening during the winter. He also told a story about running into Bigfoot while elk hunting. Another story he often told was about his encounter with what he called the Ridge Watchers.

As the story goes, he was camping in the Windrivers area, and just at dusk, they witnessed three gigantic figures at the top of the ridge looking down on his camp. Judging by the trees and other landmarks near them, they claimed they had to be at least 20 feet tall, and they were jet black.

The older I got, the more I remembered Grandpa's stories as tall tales. He passed away when I was 12, and I will never forget his stories, even if, at the time, I questioned their validity.

One summer, when I was 17, my two friends and I loaded up our horses and left to spend a week in the Windrivers. The Windrivers range is a wilderness area in Eastern Wyoming. You can go 50 miles or more and never see another soul. It's also full of breathtaking views and beautiful lakes with great fishing.

After we had traveled about 30 miles in, we decided to stop. We set up camp and hobbled the horses for the night. It was just about dusk, and my friend Tim called Ty and me over to check something out. There was a lake to the northwest of camp and a large hill to our north. He pointed up to the ridge, and there near the top, was a large black mass. None of us could remember seeing anything up there when we had arrived. The south-facing slope didn't have many tall trees, just brush. Ty quickly ran to his bedroll and came back with binoculars. After looking for a minute, he handed them to me. I adjusted them to watch, and I could see the dark outline of a head, thick neck, and shoulders. I could see the figure down to the waist, and the rest of the shadow disappeared in the brush. It was enormous! Based on deer I'd seen up on that ridge earlier and brush around it, I guessed this figure was around 15-20 feet tall, and it was deep black against the fading light.

As I was staring through the binoculars, I saw movement a short distance to the left. Two more of these giant shadows walked up next to the one that was already there. The weirdest part is that there was no detail to them; they were just intense black. We passed the binoculars back and forth until the light was gone.

We were very anxious once the light was finally gone, and we could no longer make out the forms on the hill. We built up the fire and stayed up all night. None of us wanted to sleep, knowing something so big might be out there. The night passed with no incident. With the light of the morning, the three figures were gone.

We rode to the top of the ridge that afternoon but could find no sign of footprints or anything out of place. We slept all afternoon and waited anxiously for dusk, but the figures didn't return. We enjoyed the rest of the week, fishing and exploring.

After returning home, I told my dad about what we had seen. He reminded me of Grandpa's story of the Ridge Watchers. After seeing the Ridge Watchers for myself, I'm re-thinking my earlier skepticism. Maybe Grandpa's stories were true!

John E Olsen

## PILOT MOUNTAIN MONSTER
## BY JON

My father and I were hunting Mule deer on Pilot Mountain in Utah. Pilot is a mountain in the west desert near the Nevada border, approximately 180 miles northeast of Salt Lake City, Utah.

My dad and I had been hunting all morning without much success. We had finished our PB&J lunch and had decided on a new route for our afternoon hike in hopes of finding some deer. We had just come over a small ridge when my dad spotted a mine not far down the hill. We hiked down to get a closer look. It appeared to be an ancient mine. There was some timber lying just outside the entrance. The half-buried rails looked like they might have been a part of the entry that had fallen into disrepair.

The closer we got to the entrance, the more something felt 'off' about the mine. I couldn't put my finger on exactly what I was feeling, but whatever it was, it wasn't a welcoming feeling. I began to feel like something didn't want us there. We explored the entrance carefully. Even though it was in poor shape, it seemed structurally sound. Also though we didn't have any flashlights with us, we wanted to go in just little ways to see if we could figure out what kind of mine it was.

The west desert of Utah is filled with old mines. Some are marked on area maps, and some aren't. I'd explored many mines before that day, but this one felt very different from others I'd seen. The feeling started to change to something closer to dread. I was getting a deep sense that we were walking into something we shouldn't. The eerie atmosphere was thick in the air; you could almost cut the tension with a knife.

My dad stepped in, and I followed right behind him. We only got about 15 feet inside when a sound I'd never heard before came bellowing at us from the dark. It was a deep and angry growl. The sound reverberated through my chest, out to the ends of my extremities. A long, sustained growl immediately sent me into a panic. Even though we were both armed with rifles, we turned and ran from the mine as fast as our legs would carry us. We stopped to catch our breath about 25 yards from the entrance, our hearts racing. Wide-eyed, we looked at each other, confirming that we had just heard the same thing.

We have both spent many hours out in the wilderness of Utah. We have heard many different animal sounds, and absolutely nothing we could imagine would make the terrifyingly horrible sound we experienced. We quickly left the area. We hunted the rest of the day unsuccessfully. As we got in our truck to head home, we talked about what might have been hiding just out of sight in the mine.

Nearly 25 years later…we still don't know what growled at us. I have never heard anything like what we heard just inside the mine that day.

## SKINWALKER
### BY TRINA

When I was 18 years old, I lived outside Weston, Idaho, with my Mother and Stepdad. My older sister lived in Malad, Idaho, just west of us. Every 3rd Saturday or so, I would drive over to babysit for her and her husband, then stay the night and go home Sunday morning.

I decided to just drive home late Saturday night on this particular night. It was a beautiful June night, and I felt refreshed and not at all tired. The road between Malad and Weston runs through Weston Canyon. I've driven it many times but driving it at night isn't my favorite. Driving very slowly, I made it to Weston Dam and headed through the stretch of the winding canyon road. I hadn't seen another car all night, which wasn't unusual for 1 AM in the middle of nowhere. Suddenly, as I turned a bend in the road, I saw a man standing near the side of the road. As my headlight hit him, I noticed he had long white hair and a dirty red blanket over his shoulders. In his hand was a walking stick and his eyes seemed to glow red like deer eyes in the light. I slowed down, and as I passed, I could see he had the complexion of an old Native American man; he also seemed to be snarling at me like a mad dog. I was instantly freaked out and continued driving a little faster. I knew there were sheepherders up here, and I convinced myself it must have been one of them.

I had traveled about half a mile down the road, and my heart had calmed down when, as I turned on the last turns in the canyon, my headlights shined on another man. As I drove closer, my blood turned to ice as I realized it was the same old man. He had the same dirty red blanket and crazy white hair. He held the same walking stick. As my headlight hit him, he had the same wild, an angry snarl on his face. I quickly accelerated past the man and headed out of the canyon

I woke up my Mom and cried for 10 minutes before I could calm down enough to talk. By the time I got home, I was in hysterics. My mom thought it was just someone playing a prank, but I was convinced it was something else.

It's been many years, and I still will not drive that road alone. After some study, I believe it was a Skinwalker, a Native American witch of legend. Whatever it was, it wanted to harm me, and I believe this in my heart.

Beyond Stranger Bridgerland

John E Olsen

## THE SMILING MAN
### BY JACOB

It wasn't until a while after my encounter that I found out I wasn't the only person that had met the Smiling Man.

It was the fall of 1988, and I was 19 years old. I had planned on deer hunting with my dad, but he had come down with the stomach flu the day before. I decided to go by myself, so I packed up my old car and left early Saturday morning before dawn. I stopped at a point near the summit of Logan canyon right before you drop into the Bear Lake Valley. I waited until it was light enough to shoot and headed south down the ridge. I got to a place where I could watch several spots where deer might run if scared by other hunters. I knew there were hunters to the west towards 'The Sinks', so my best bet of shooting a deer was sitting and waiting.

I sat until about 10 am. I'd seen a few doe's and small bucks but nothing I wanted to shoot. I was thinking about walking further south along the ridge when I spotted someone in the clearing below me. I looked with my binoculars, and to my surprise, standing in the middle of the clearing was a very tall man. The clearing was about 200 yards below me, and I knew he hadn't been there just moments before. He was standing with his back to me, not moving. He had on a pale-yellow suit with a black pinstripe hat like you'd see on a man in the '50s. He held a briefcase in his left hand and looked to be staring at the sun.

I was dumbfounded. I knew the man wasn't there

moments before because I had just scanned that area. I watched him intently with my binoculars for about 10 minutes, deciding what to do. During that time, he never moved a muscle.

I loaded up my pack and headed down toward the man, keeping him in my sight at all times. I had a bizarre feeling as I hiked down to him. As I entered the clearing, I decided to make a little noise as I approached not to startle him. I made heavy footsteps and purposely walked on a few branches, but he remained as still as a statue. As I got closer, I noticed a strange smell in the air. It was a light sulfur ozone smell. I could tell he was a good six and a half feet or taller; he was bald under his hat and pale complexion. I got about 15 feet from him, and I asked if he was ok. He jumped just a little, then turned to look at me. He had bright blue eyes and an unusual smile across his face. His eyes and face sent shivers through my body. After a moment, I asked again if he was ok.

He looked at me and said, "I've seemed to have misplaced myself."
"You're lost?" I replied.
"Lost? Yes, lost," he said. "Can you point me to the nearest settlement?"

I wanted to run as fast as I could from him. The strange man spoke broken English as if it was not his first language. I pulled myself together and pointed east. I told him Lake Town was 4 miles or so east of here. He tipped his hat to me, turned, and walked towards the town. After he disappeared into the trees, I came back to my senses. The entire incident felt very hazy, and I felt extremely uneasy. I managed to make my way back to my car in a daze. When I got there, I looked at my watch. It was just after 4 pm. I was so confused because I knew I had first spotted the man at about 10 am. The hike down, talking to him, and the hike back shouldn't have taken 6 hours. I drove home and told my dad what had happened. He suggested I keep it to myself.

I've since read stories of the Smiling Man and his connection with UFOs. To this day, I can still picture his face, and it still haunts me.

John E Olsen

## LATE-NIGHT VISITOR
### BY KARRIN

I live in a small town outside Preston, Idaho. I've lived there since the late 1960s. My husband and I raised two sons in a small older home just on the edge of town. Not a lot happens in our quiet little town, except for this one night that I will never forget.

It was in the mid-'80s, and my sons were 8 and 11 at the time. We had all gone to bed around 9 o'clock that night as usual. It was an early crisp summer night in June with a full moon with no cloud in the sky. I remember how beautiful it was as I took a trash bag outside right before I headed to bed.

I woke up at 2 am to the dogs barking up a storm. Skunks or raccoons would often wander through the cornfield, setting off the dogs. After about 10 minutes of barking, I was just about to get up to yell at them when they both yelped and stopped barking. The yelp sounded like they were frightened or hurt. The yelp isn't a sound they had ever made before. I lay in bed listening for a few minutes but couldn't sleep, so I crawled out and slipped on my robe. My husband was softly snoring away on his side of the bed. He could sleep through anything! I groggily walked to the back door, turned on the porch light, and opened the door. I could see both dogs cowering in the doghouse. Joe, our big black lab, was whimpering, and Soups, our little mutt, was hiding under Joe. There was a horrible smell in the air-like wet garbage and musty animal. I figured they had been sprayed by a skunk and hid in their house.

I shut and locked the back door and went to the kitchen.

I turned on the light and went to the sink to get a drink before heading to bed. As I filled my glass, I looked out the window to the front yard. I couldn't see clearly because of the glare on the glass from the light, but I could see a figure standing by the pine tree out front. I ran over and turned off the light. I slowly approached the window. Standing by the pine tree was an enormous man or creature. The moon was at his back so that I couldn't see the details of his face, but he was tall - around 8 feet or more. The figure had a very short, muscular neck and a head that came up to a point. One large arm fell to his side while the other pulled needles off the pine tree.

I stared at him for what seemed like forever, and I could feel him staring at me. Finally, coming to my senses, I backed out of the kitchen and ran to the bedroom. By the time I reached the bedroom, I was shrieking. My husband jumped from the bed, startled by my outburst. I told him I saw a man in the front yard. He grabbed his shotgun, threw on a coat, and headed to the front door. I followed behind him with a flashlight I grabbed from my nightstand. We ran out the front door and found nothing. The stench loomed in the air as we walked to the tree. A small pile of pine needles and limbs sat on the grass under the tree.

My husband asked if he should call the sheriff. I told him I didn't know what I would say to them. It took some time before I felt comfortable getting up at night again. After many years of going over it in my mind, I believe that I saw Bigfoot that night.

## HALLOWEEN IN WELLSVILLE
### BY ANTHONY

I was a Senior in High School in the early '90s. I lived between Hyrum and Wellsville, Utah, at the time. It was the week of Halloween, and I had just taken my girlfriend, Tiffany, on a date. We stopped by my house so she could say hello to my parents before taking Tiffany home. We stayed a little longer than expected, so it was around 11 o'clock when we left to take her home. She lived in Tremonton, and I knew the route well. I would drive through Wellsville, then along Valley View Highway, to Tremonton. As we headed into Wellsville, we talked about scary stories because it was two days before Halloween. I decided to take a slight detour into the Wellsville Cemetery to scare Tiffany. I figured it would be funny until I had pulled into the first lane in the cemetery, and my headlights came upon a scene I'll never forget.

In the road in front of us that ran down the south side of the cemetery was a large moving van. Lining the road on both sides of the van was about 10-15 people in dark brown robes with full hoods covering their heads and faces. As soon as my headlights shined on the road, they stopped what they were doing. We were frozen, staring for what seemed like forever. The hooded strangers were looking back at us motionless. We all stared at each other, not moving. I suddenly felt Tiffany's hand on my shoulder as she whispered. "We have to go."

I immediately put the car in reverse, and instantly, the hooded figures began to run after us. Tiffany screamed as I raced backward out of the cemetery. I felt like I had stepped into a horror movie. I hit the road at the bottom and sped off, headed for Main Street in Wellsville. I found a payphone and called the county dispatch. My brother-in-law was a dispatcher at the time, and I happened to get him on the line. I explained what we had seen, and they immediately sent an officer to check it out. Later my brother-in-law told me they found nothing at the cemetery. After dropping off Tiffany and heading home, it was nearly 2 am by the time I pulled in.

I found out later that the same group of hooded people had visited three other cemeteries in the valley, but no one could figure out what they were doing. I still get creeped out when I think about it and what it could have been.

## LIGHTS OUTHOUSE
### BY TERRY

In the early '80s, my church purchased the land above the Porcupine dam. It is in the mountains at the southeast end of Cache Valley, just above the town of Avon, Utah.

At the time, it was very undeveloped. It was very primitive camping with a few outhouses here and there. One Saturday, I was asked to take a few boys from our church group and do some cleanup. They wanted us also to take stock of what needed to be done that summer. I took two young men with me that had volunteered and headed out there just after noon on a beautiful Saturday in May.

We drove the rocky road up and around Porcupine Dam. We stopped at the top of the canyon and began clearing some brush, checking the outhouses for snakes and animals. We brought supplies to make dinner and marshmallows to roast after working. Once we finished, we got a fire going, and we ate and talked until well past dark.

Finally, it was time to go home. We put out the fire, loaded up the truck, and headed down the canyon. We laughed and had a good time telling stories when we rounded the bend to a wide-open spot in the canyon where we could see three outhouses from the road. I slammed on my breaks, and we skidded to a halt. The sight before us made us all speechless. It was very dark, the moon had not come up yet, but the little field was clearly visible because of the strange light coming from all three outhouses. Each outhouse had a brilliant bright light glowing from inside. It was so bright that the cracks in the doors and in between the boards on the sides shot bright beams across the brush. It looked like each one had a spotlight inside. The younger boy spoke up in a quiet squeaky voice. "Did we forget to turn off the lights in the outhouses?"

It was quiet for a moment, and I replied, "There are no lights in them; there isn't even any electricity here."

I had no idea what was causing the lights in the outhouses. Nothing anyone could have hauled up here was that bright. We hadn't seen another person all day. I rolled down my window, and all I could hear was my truck engine; there were no other sounds. I debated whether to go look or not when the boys asked if we could leave in unison. A deep feeling of unrest hit me, and I realized that I didn't want to know what was in there. I drove off at a quick but safe speed. Miles later, after we got to the paved road, the silence in the car was interrupted by the boys asking what I thought we had seen. I didn't have a clue, and I still don't. I know it was brilliantly bright and scared me, whatever it was.

## GOLFING WITH BIGFOOT
### BY JON

I grew up in Hyde Park, Utah, just north of Logan, UT. When I was a kid, I spent a lot of time with my buddy Trevor. He lived in Smithfield, the next town over. One of the things we liked to do was ride up to the golf course to find golf balls. On one occasion, our golf ball hunt took a strange turn.

I remember being 12 years old. It was a Saturday evening at the end of April. We rode our bikes up to the golf course and made our way toward the big gully that divided the golf course in half. It's about 85 yards wide and full of brush and trees. The gully was one of our favorite places to search because three different holes required golfers to shoot over it.

We were starting to have trouble seeing because it was getting late. We looked around, and there wasn't anyone else around to hassle us. We watched our steps as we worked our way into the gully. I spotted something significant laying by some thick brush. As I got closer, I realized it was a dead deer. I yelled to Trevor and walked closer to take a better look. It had not been dead very long and was lying on its side. The weirdest part was that its head was twisted backward, a full 180 degrees. I was staring at the deer, wondering what could have done that to a deer. I heard Trevor walking down the hill towards me.

I looked up to see him, and he stopped dead in his tracks. Instantly, all the blood left his face, and his eyes were the size of dinner plates. He motioned at me to come towards him, and then he turned and ran out of the gully at full speed. Without looking around me, I took off after him. I caught up to him at the top of the hill, and I grabbed his shirt to stop him. After catching our breath, he explained that as I was standing by the deer, a sizeable hairy arm had reached through the brush and was just about to grab me.

I was beginning to question whether he had really seen an arm when a loud guttural scream came from the gully out of nowhere. We looked down into the fading light just in time to see an enormous hairy blur rush through the trees below us. In an instant, we had run across the course and were racing away on our bikes, scared to death, afraid it was coming our way. We made it to Trevor's house in record time. Still out of breath, we tried to explain what had happened to our family, but no one believed us. Even at school, no one listened to our story.

Trevor and I, to this day, are 100% convinced we came face to face with a Sasquatch that day at the golf course.

John E Olsen

## WELLSVILLE MOUNTAIN MONSTER
### BY TRAVIS

My friend Tyler and I had decided we wanted to hike the Wellsville mountains. We were both in our 30s and lived in the valley for most of our lives but had never hiked them. Neither of us where in bad shape, but the Wellsville mountains are a long steep climb, and we wanted to be ready. We prepared for most of the summer by doing smaller hikes and just walking town with our wives.

We had chosen a Friday to Saturday climb. You can do it in a single day, but we wanted to enjoy the experience, and camping out on the mountain sounded fun. We left early and parked at the entrance to the trail just above Mendon, Utah. The path is 11 miles, and the hike gains

4,669 feet in elevation. It's listed as a moderate hike, but it's not for the faint-hearted.

We headed out planning on making it to the top by 1 pm. Then we could spend the day taking pictures and looking for fossils. As we climbed to the top, we could see all of Cache Valley. The first half is in many trees, and you don't see much, but after that, the trees become scarcer, and the view is spectacular. The rest of the day was beautiful. We hiked and explored, finding fossils and watching wildlife. As it got to be later in the afternoon, we found a spot just off a ridge to make camp. We set up our tent and ate dinner. We stayed up, enjoying the view of the lights in the valley and the stars. Around 10 PM, the wind picked up, and we headed to bed.

Sometime during the night, I woke up, something was very wrong, but I didn't know what. I was trying to clear my head when I heard a strange sound. I realized it was tranquil with no sounds except this deep thumping. After a moment, I realized it sounded like heavy footsteps. Whatever it was, it was on two feet. The creature was coming down the trail and towards our tent. I slipped out of my sleeping bag and peeked through the tent flap. It was foggy, and I couldn't see much outside. The deep footsteps got closer and closer. As it arrived within a few yards of us, I held my breath. Suddenly the footfall stopped. The only sound I could hear now was the pounding of my heart in my ears. After what felt like forever, the creature started moving again. This time it turned down to the right of us and headed down the hill. I listened to the heavy footsteps until they disappeared down the mountain. I heard a few large trees break below us. The sound of it echoed through the still air, then silence.

I was still straining to hear any noises when Tyler asked. "What was that?"

I just about jumped out of my skin! I'd been listening so hard for sounds that I had forgotten he was even there. I told him I had no idea and explained I couldn't see it through the fog.

Once it was light out, we threw our packs together and made our way out. We both agreed it was something huge and that it was walking on 2 feet, but we couldn't speculate beyond that. I've never been one to believe in Sasquatch, but after that night, I'm not that sure.

# John E Olsen

## BLACKEYES AT MIDNIGHT
### BY KIMBERLY

My parents had gone on a vacation for a week; they asked me to house sit while they were away. They lived in a lovely house in a small town outside of Tremonton. I was 21 and lived in an old apartment; I was working and going to school in Ogden, Utah, and was excited to have a beautiful place to stay for a week.

It was a very uneventful week until Friday night. I had been busy all week and wanted nothing more than to eat some takeout and watch my favorite movie. I ate dinner and locked up the house. I lay down on the couch and started watching TV. At some point, I fell asleep.

I woke up to a banging on the front door. I was groggy, and it took a moment to pull myself together. The banging on the front door came again. As I became more coherent, I questioned who was banging and why they were not using the doorbell. I got to the door and tried to flip on the porch light, but nothing happened. I looked out the window and was shocked to see two little girls standing on my porch. I wanted to get a better look at who it was, so I flipped the light in the front room. It lit the porch just enough so that I could tell they were alone.

I opened the door but left the screen door closed. "Can I help you?" I asked. The girls appeared to be wearing what looked like homemade dresses. One seemed to be about 7 or 8, and the other was around 11. Their hair was long and was hanging in their face, and their head was down, so it was hard to see their faces. After a moment, the little one asked: "Can we come into your house?"

I quickly replied, "No, what are you doing out here?" I had a horrible feeling about this entire situation.

"Our mother got a flat up the road; she'll be coming to get us soon. Can't we come into your house?" I explained it was late and that it wasn't going to happen. The little one kept insisting they needed into the house.

I was closing the door with a firm "NO!" When the older girl took a step forward.

"You have to invite us in! We're just little girls!" She said this with a forceful tone. As she stepped forward, I got a better look at her face and her eyes. These little girls had jet black eyes.

I slammed the door and locked it. The kids stepped off the porch and just stood facing the house. After a few horrific minutes, I was just about to grab the phone to call 911 when an old black car came rolling up the driveway. I didn't see which direction it had come from. The girls climbed into the car, and it drove away. I sat up the rest of the night, afraid to go to bed.

The following day, I went outside to see what was wrong

with the front porch light. But when I hit the switch, it turned on like normal. Saturday was the last night at the house, so I asked one of my friends to spend the night at the house with me. Nothing happened that night, and the children didn't return. It wasn't until I heard of the black-eyed kids a few years later. It was good to know I wasn't alone, but I'll never forget the night I saw them.

John E Olsen

## GLITCHES IN THE MATRIX

The term "Glitch in the Matrix" explains something that happens to you that simply can't be explained under normal circumstances. Glitches can include anything from seeing something that doesn't make sense to a skip in time. Though this has been happening as far back as written time, the phrase has only been used since the turn of the century. It comes from the movie "The Matrix," where humanity lives inside a computer-generated world. I've been lucky to collect several stories that fall under a "Glitch in the Matrix." It seems there is more and more all the time.

## A SKIP BACK
### BY BLAKE

I have a nightly routine I follow every night. It doesn't change because it helps me ensure I get everything done. I'm a little OCD when it comes to my routine. I hate getting in bed to remember I've forgotten to do something.

As I got ready for bed one night, my wife was in bed already reading. I had locked the doors, checked the cat's food and water then proceeded to the bedroom. I showered, took my medicine, and took my CPAP water reservoir over to the dresser, where I kept my purified water. I opened my new jug of water, filled it, and walked back to the bed stand, placing the reservoir back in my CPAP machine.

I was just about to turn off the light when there was a knock at the bedroom door. My 15-year-old daughter was asking about a ride in the morning. I answered her and went to shut off the light when I noticed my reservoir was not in my CPAP machine. Puzzled, I looked and saw it was sitting on the dresser open. I walked over to it to find it was empty. Now more confused, I looked at the jug of water to see it was still sealed, sitting unopened. I went over what had just happened in my mind, knowing full well I had opened that jug and filled my CPAP. After a few moments, my wife looked up and said: "Didn't you already fill that?" I explained what had happened, and she looked perplexed. She said she remembered me filling up the CPAP and locking it in, just as I had.

It's two years later, it's never happened again, but I am still dumbfounded about how everything seemed to reset.

## I SAW "ME"
### BY JACKSON

In the spring of 2010, I was a junior at Utah State. It was a warm spring day, and I wanted to study outside for my finals. I lived just off-campus and rode my bike everywhere. I had an old Toyota pickup, but I only took that if I traveled out of town.

It was about noon on a Friday before the week of finals, so traffic was light as I biked up to campus. I remember a few people playing frisbee just to the east of me, and there was a little foot traffic coming and going. I decided to take a blanket and sit out on the quad just east of Old Main. Overall, it was a beautiful day.

I was deep into reading my chemistry notes when I realized someone had stopped on the sidewalk in front of me. I looked up and let my eyes adjust to my surroundings. I expected to see a friend or someone I knew, but what I saw made my breath catch in my throat.

Standing in front of me was ME! He looked as shocked as I felt. It took a moment for my brain to catch up with my eyes. He was wearing jean shorts just like me and a gray shirt with no logo, the same as I was wearing. Looking at his face was like looking in a mirror. The only real difference was his hat. I've always been a massive fan of the Seattle Seahawks football team, and I was wearing my favorite Seahawks hat. He was also wearing a hat with the Seahawks logo, but the colors were wrong. Instead of blue and green, it was a blue and red color that didn't seem to match. He was walking a bike that looked like the one sitting on the grass next to me.

I sat confused for what seemed like an eternity. Suddenly my doppelganger seemed to snap out of a trance and threw his backpack (that looked just like mine) over his shoulder, hopped on his bike he took off. I snapped out of my daze and called out to him. Before zipping out of sight behind the Old Main building, he looked over his shoulder. I left my blanket and books and jumped on my bike to follow him. I rode all over campus for an hour but found no sign of him.

I was still shaken up when I made it back to my blanket. I gathered my stuff and headed back to my apartment. I've gone over this incident in my head millions of times. Who was that person walking on campus that day? Was he from another dimension? I still have no clue who or what I witnessed that day.

## HOME AGAIN
### BY ANN

My husband and I lived in our first home outside of Cedar City in southern Utah. He had just finished college and worked for a small company in town. I was working part-time and going to school. I was trying to finish up my degree.

My story detailed three different occasions when I had strange experiences in our home...

The first incident happened when I was folding laundry in my bedroom. It was around 5 pm, and I expected my husband to be home anytime. We had an appointment at 6:30 to meet friends for dinner. I was almost done folding when I heard the front door open. I listened to my husband yell out, "I made it! I'm home!" Then he dropped his keys in his usual spot; a bowl by the door. I called out, letting him know I was in the bedroom, but he didn't respond. After a minute or two, I walked down the short hallway to the front room to say hello. But, instead of finding my husband, I found the house empty and quiet. There were no keys in the bowl. I walked to the kitchen to look for him, but he wasn't in there either. I walked outside, and his car was gone. Confused, I walked back into the bedroom and put the clothes away.

I was almost done when I heard the front door open. Once again listened to my husband call out, "I made it! I'm home!" and listened to his keys rattle as they hit the bowl. I walked into the front room very confused. This time my husband was there, standing by the door looking at the mail. I stood there puzzled for a moment and asked where he had been. He looked up and met my eyes; his expression was now as confused as mine. He explained that he had come straight home from work and had not been home until just that moment. I explained what I had heard. Neither of us could figure out what had happened.

I brushed the incident off until about a month later. It was a Sunday evening, and my husband rushed off to a Church meeting right after dinner. I watched some television and then decided to head to bed to read. Around 8:45 pm, I heard the door open, and my hubby came in. He tossed his keys in the bowl with a clang and called out a cheery "Hello!" I called out to him, "I'm in bed; how did it go?" I heard two or three footsteps approaching my bedroom from down the hall, then silence. I called out, "Hello! I'm in the bedroom!" But I got no answer-back. I rolled out of bed and walked out of my room to find an empty hallway. I walked into the central part of the house; nothing. I was pretty unnerved. I walked back to the bedroom and sat at the end of my bed, figuring out what was going on. After about 15 minutes, the door opened, and the scene played out again. My husband called out, the keys hit the bowl, and more footsteps came down the hall. But this time, he was actually home, and he walked back into the bedroom to see me. I explained what had happened. Again, we had no explanation.

About a month later, I was in the bathtub soaking one night. My husband had gone to play basketball ball with some of his friends. I thought I heard my husband come home. I heard all the usual sounds. I listened to the front door open and shut, and once again, the keys hitting the bowl. I apprehensively listened for any indication of whether he was really home or not. The bathroom wasn't too far from the kitchen. I heard him walk in and get a glass of water. I called out, "How was the game!?" I was met with silence. I called out again but got no answer. I sat in the tub, straining to hear anything, but there were no more sounds to be heard. I was just about to get out of the tub to look around the house when the door opened again. All the same, sounds played out precisely as they had before. Hesitantly, I called out, "Honey is that you?" I was comforted when my husband's voice came through the wall, "Yep! I just got home!" After getting out of the tub, I broke down. I explained what had happened. This time I was afraid he was going to think I was crazy! He held me and got me calmed down. We talked it through, and even though it was very unusual, I felt like he believed me.

Not long after that third incident, I graduated, and we moved out of that house. It hasn't happened since. Looking back, I believe it was some sort of auditory skip in time. I know that sounds unrealistic, but that's the best explanation I can come up with for my weird story.

John E Olsen

## BEAR LAKE

Bear Lake lies 41 miles East of Logan, Utah. The Lake itself is believed to be 250,000 years old. It was discovered in 1818 by fur trappers but has been used by the Shoshone Tribe for much longer. The Shoshone and many other Native American Tribes would trade furs for supplies brought in by the fur companies. They traded in Rendezvous, near what is now called Laketown. Years later, in 1863, Mormon pioneers from Salt Lake City settled in the Bear Lake Valley.

Stories of the Bear Lake Monster have been told around many campfires for years. Rumors circulated of the Shoshone seeing the Monster before white men arrived.

Sightings of the Monster have dwindled over the years, but the oldest stories are still told. A settler of the Bear Lake Valley wrote two accounts of unusual events that happened to him while growing up in the area. These are his stories:

## LOGS IN THE WATER

The best way to get logs around at the time was to float them on the lake. At 16 years of age, it was my job to find the logs onshore and drag them further up with the horses to be loaded and taken to the mill. One morning, I spotted three logs just offshore on the east side of Bear Lake. I brought the two horses down and hooked them up to the logs. Then, I drove the horses to the top of the hill just above the shore. I unhitched the logs and looked back at the water. There, right near the beach, were two more logs. I cursed under my breath for not seeing them before and hooked the leads back up to my horses. As we got to the bottom of the hill, I realized that what I saw were not logs at all. They were two enormous fish-type creatures. They had dark scaly skin and large eyes; both were easily over 7 feet long. Suddenly with a splash, they both disappeared into the depths of the water.

## FLYING BALL

It was late September, and I had been logging on the East side of the Bear Lake valley. It was just after midday. I was sitting at the bottom of a vast canyon, enjoying the lunch my mother had packed. I could see perfectly across the lake because it was a clear day.

Suddenly, the bugs and birds stopped making noises, and they became very still. I began to hear a bizarre sound. It was a very high-pitched squealing noise that was rising higher and higher. It continued until it became so high, I could not hear it anymore, but I could still feel it in my chest. The horses started to whine because the sound was hurting their ears. The sounds were starting to hurt my ears too.

Suddenly, there was a giant ball of light from above me on the hill just above the tree line. It came up from behind the farthest trees above the canyon. It was gold and flashed red all over like nothing anyone could imagine. It floated in midair and looked to be the size of a large house. Then it floated down the canyon. It passed right over my head and out across the lake. It looked as if it would hit the mountain on the west side but suddenly shot up in a flash and was gone. The sounds of the forest returned, and the horses quickly calmed down. I've never seen anything like it before or since.

John E Olsen

## HARDWARE RANCH LOST GOLD

Growing up in Hyrum Ut and being from a family that helped settle Cache Valley, I heard many stories about this beautiful area. One story my grandpa told me was about the Lost Gold near Hardware Ranch.

During the Gold Rush in California, two miners from the eastern United States had traveled to the west coast to seek their fortune. They had arrived in the California Goldfields and did indeed strike it rich. After a few years, they decided to return to the east with their riches and gold. They loaded up a mule train and headed east for home.

Unfortunately, they left a little late in the season and were attempting a trek through northern Utah to get to Wyoming.

They traveled through Cache Valley and through Blacksmith Fork just east of Hyrum, Utah. Sadly, a terrible winter storm hit about 14 miles into the mountains. Their mules were dying, and they were unprepared for such cold weather, so they hid the gold and tried to make it down to Ogden, Utah. On their way, one of the miners froze to death. Nearly dead, the last miner made it to Ogden, where he spent the winter recovering.

The last miner hired a few men to help recover his gold in the spring. He would only tell them roughly where it was. It's somewhere between Hardware Ranch and an area we now call Ant Flats. As the men made their way to the location, they ran into a band of Shoshone, and an altercation ensued. The last miner was killed during the fight. He died, taking the exact location of the gold to his grave.

A few of the men in the party looked for years but never found it. Many have tried and failed to find the lost gold throughout the years. Today, most or possibly all the land is now on private property and blocked off to the public. The gold is estimated to be worth millions in today's market.

## ABOUT THE AUTHOR

John Olsen lives in Hyrum, Utah, in beautiful Cache Valley with his wife and three children. He has spent 30+ years researching and collecting paranormal stories for this book series. John is still collecting stories and would love to hear from you. You can contact him at olsenj243@gmail.com

Look for other books from Author John Olsen
Stranger Bridgerland
Beyond Stranger Bridgerland
Stranger West
Stranger U.S
Beyond Stranger U.S
Check out
www.strangerbridgerland.com

Made in United States
North Haven, CT
09 November 2022